This anthology has been made possible
with financial assistance from
The John S. Cohen Foundation

Published by the South Bank Centre,
London SE1 8XX

Classification: Poetry
ISBN: 0954480708

With Thanks to Ruth Borthwick and Sasha Hoare,
Literature + Talks, Royal Festival Hall.

fifty fifty

ANTHOLOGY

Fifty Poems from Fifty Years of the Poetry Library

1953 - 2003

Edited by
Charles Bainbridge
Tania Earnshaw
Selima Hill
Mimi Khalvati
Stephen Knight
Simon Smith

Fifty Years of the Poetry Library

1953 The Arts Council Poetry Library opens at the National Book League, Albemarle Street, London W1. Speakers at the opening are T. S. Eliot and Herbert Read. The Library is founded on the recommendation of the Poetry Panel of the Arts Council of Great Britain. Coverage is from 1930 to the present.

1969 Library moves to the premises of the Arts Council of Great Britain, 105 Piccadilly, London W1.

1973 At this time the collection includes 6,000 titles. Start date of the collection is newly set at poetry published from 1912 to the present day from the English-speaking world. Contemporary poetry translated into English from other languages forms an increasing part of the collection. Contemporary poetry magazines collection begins. A trebling of book stock and growth in use of the resource leads to the next move.

1978 Library moves to 9 Long Acre, London WC2, reopened by Charles Osborne, Literature Director of the Arts Council. Holdings of pre-twentieth-century poetry translated into English by contemporary English language poets, recordings of poets reading their work and poetry for children strengthened. "The Noticeboard of Lost Quotations" created. Noticeable increase in library use by anthologists, such as Seamus Heaney and Ted Hughes, who research *The Rattle Bag* in the Library.

'50s | '60s | '70s

1962 Penguin Modern Poets series launched with a volume by Lawrence Durrell, Elizabeth Jennings and R.S. Thomas.
1965 T.S. Eliot dies. Plath's *Ariel* published. Royal Albert Hall poetry reading.
1967 *Penguin Modern Poets 10: Mersey Sound* includes poems by Adrian Henri, Roger McGough and Brian Patten. Poetry International started by Ted Hughes.
1968 Northern Poetry Library founded in Morpeth. Cecil Day Lewis made Poet Laureate.
1969 *Children of Albion* anthology published.

1972 John Betjeman new Poet Laureate. The Poetry Society starts the Poets in Schools scheme.
1973 *Poetry Nation One* published by Michael Schmidt and C.B. Cox; later becomes the magazine *PN Review* then *PNR*.
1975 All Ezra Pound's *Cantos* published.
1976 *Bluefoot Traveller: Poetry by West Indians* in Britain published. Sorley MacLean's *Roethairt is Contraigh/Spring Tide and Neap Tide* appears.
1977 Eric Mottram's editorship of *Poetry Review* comes to an end.
1978 First Bloodaxe Books publications.
1979 Seamus Heaney's *Field Work* published.

1953 Poetry Book Society formed. Death of Dylan Thomas.
1955 Publication of *The Less Deceived* by Philip Larkin.
1959 William Cookson publishes the first *Agenda*.

1983 Library moves to the
premises of the Arts Council of
Great Britain, 105 Piccadilly,
London W1, reopened by Lord
Gowrie, the Arts Minister.
At this time the collection includes
over 30,000 titles.**1988** Library
moves to present location within
the South Bank Centre, opened by
Seamus Heaney. Renamed the
Saison Poetry Library housing the
Arts Council Poetry Collection.

1991 Library catalogue goes online.
1993 Fortieth Birthday
celebrations introduced by Sir
Stephen Spender, with a reading by
John Agard.

2002 Start of the magazine
digitalisation project.
2002-3 New extension to the
Library built to expand the
reference, study and children's
areas. Collection now numbers
60,000 items, with over 20,000
members of the library.

'80s   '90s   '00s

1980 Paul Muldoon's *Why
Brownlee Left* published.
1982 *Penguin Book of
Contemporary Poetry* edited by
Blake Morrison and Andrew
Motion. Apples and Snakes' first
poetry cabaret.
1983 Valerie Bloom's *Touch Mi,
Tell Mi* published.
1984 Ted Hughes new Poet
Laureate.
News from Babylon edited by
James Berry. Founding of the
Scottish Poetry Library.
1985 *Bloodaxe Book of
Contemporary Women Poets*
edited by Jeni Couzyn.
Death of Philip Larkin.
1986 First *Poems on the
Underground.*
1987 *A Various Art* published by
Carcanet. Televised version of
Tony Harrison's *V* broadcast.
1988 *new british poetry* published
by Paladin Grafton. Re-launch of
Poetry International at the South
Bank Centre.

1990 First Signal Poetry Award to
Allan Ahlberg for *Heard It in the
Playground.*
1992 First Forward Poetry Prize
for best collection awarded to
Thom Gunn for *The Man With
Night Sweats.*
1993 First T.S. Eliot Poetry Prize
awarded to Ciaran Carson for *First
Language. The New Poetry*
anthology published by Bloodaxe.
1994 First National Poetry Day.
New Generation promotion
brings widespread attention to
20 new poets.
1995 Seamus Heaney is awarded
the Nobel Prize.
1996 Poetry Olympics weekend at
the Royal Albert Hall.
1998 Death of Ted Hughes.
1999 Andrew Motion new
Poet Laureate.

2001 Anne Carson the first woman
to win the T.S. Eliot Poetry Prize.

5

Introduction

The first reaction of many readers when they pick up an anthology is to ask how the editor(s) went about choosing the contents. The central aim of this book was to reflect the holdings and character of the Poetry Library. The idea was not to look for another re-writing of the history of poetry, the promotion of one group or movement, or a polemic. We wanted to create an anthology which was inclusive and celebratory; a book that would revel in the great qualities of late twentieth and early twenty-first century poetry – its wide range and vast scope, its democracy, in short.

There were six editors – three members of the Poetry Library staff (Charles Bainbridge, Tania Earnshaw and myself) and three poets (Selima Hill, Mimi Khalvati and Stephen Knight) who have worked closely with the library and know it well. Each chose a list of poems published over the last fifty years that were important to them. The criteria were simple: the poems had to come from a book in the Poetry Library, written or translated into English in the last fifty years and to be, in most cases, under a page in length. Each poet was allowed no more than one poem in the book.

With six editors and over a hundred poems to discuss, the process was by turns humorous, heated and sometimes a little arbitrary. We went through each year at a time, voting for the poem we thought best. Some years there were six contenders, some years only two. If there was a tie (which happened frequently) lots were drawn. The only year this committee of readers was unanimous about was 1975 (Cavafy). The process to a great extent, therefore, chose the poems and while the anthology contains poems that each editor individually put forward it also contains poems that not every editor would like to see there. Despite this or rather because of it, the resulting book, I think, provides a strangely balanced selection of work.

What we present here, I believe, reflects poetry from the last fifty years: quirky, funny, serious, simple and sophisticated, accessible and difficult, experimental and traditional – and all available in book form on the shelves of the Poetry Library.

Simon Smith
Librarian
The Poetry Library

CONTENTS

1953

Wind in the Street

The same faces, and then the same scandals
Confront me inside the talking shop which I
Frequent for my own good. So the assistant
Points to the old cogwheels, the old handles
Set in machines which to buy would be to buy
The same faces, and then the same scandals.

I climb by the same stairs to a square attic.
And I gasp, for surely this is something new!
So square, so simple. It is new to be so simple.
Then I see the same sky through the skylight, static
Cloudless, the same artificial toylike blue.
The same stairs led to the same attic.

I only came, I explain, to look round,
To the assistant who coos while I regain the street.
Searching thoroughly, I did not see what I wanted.
What I wanted would have been what I found.
My voice carries, his voice blows to his feet:
I only came, I explain, to look round.

I may return, meanwhile I'll look elsewhere:
My want may modify to what I have seen.
So I smile wearily, though even as I smile
A purposeful gust of wind tugs at my hair;
But I turn, I wave, I am not sure what I mean.
I may return, meanwhile I'll look elsewhere.

Thom Gunn

The Poem That Took the Place of a Mountain

There it was, word for word,
The poem that took the place of a mountain.

He breathed its oxygen,
Even when the book lay turned in the dust of his table.

It reminded him how he had needed
A place to go to in his own direction,

How he had recomposed the pines,
Shifted the rocks and picked his way among clouds,

For the outlook that would be right,
Where he would be complete in an unexplained completion:

The exact rock where his inexactnesses
Would discover, at last, the view toward which they had edged,

Where he could lie and, gazing down at the sea,
Recognize his unique and solitary home.

Wallace Stevens

1955

Chinese Ballad

Now he has seen the girl Hsiang-Hsiang,
　　Now back to the guerrilla band;
And she goes with him down the vale
　　And pauses at the strand.

The mud is yellow, deep, and thick,
　　And their feet stick, where the stream turns.
'Make me two models out of this,
　　That clutches as it yearns.

'Make one of me and one of you,
　　And both shall be alive.
Were there no magic in the dolls
　　The children could not thrive.

'When you have made them smash them back:
　　They yet shall live again.
Again make dolls of you and me
　　But mix them grain by grain.

'So your flesh shall be part of mine
　　And part of mine be yours.
Brother and sister we shall be
　　Whose unity endures.

'Always the sister doll will cry,
　　Made in these careful ways,
Cry on and on, Come back to me,
　　Come back, in a few days.'

William Empson

The Sycamore

Against a gun-metal sky
I saw an albino giraffe. Without
leaves to modify,
chamois-white as
said, although partly pied near the base,
it towered where a chain of
stepping-stones lay in a stream nearby;
glamour to stir the envy

of anything in motley –
Hampshire pig, the living lucky-stone; or
all-white butterfly.
A commonplace:
there's more than just one kind of grace.
We don't like flowers that do
not wilt; they must die, and nine
she-camel-hairs aid memory.

Worthy of Imami,
the Persian – clinging to a stiffer stalk
was a little dry
thing from the grass,
in the shape of a Maltese cross,
retiringly formal
as if to say: "And there was I
like a field-mouse at Versailles."

Marianne Moore

I Remember

It was my bridal night I remember,
An old man of seventy-three
I lay with my young bride in my arms,
A girl with t.b.
It was wartime, and overhead
The Germans were making a particularly heavy raid on Hampstead.
What rendered the confusion worse, perversely
Our bombers had chosen that moment to set out for Germany.
Harry, do they ever collide?
I do not think it has ever happened,
Oh my bride, my bride.

Stevie Smith

I Knew A Woman

I knew a woman, lovely in her bones,
When small birds sighed, she would sigh back at them;
Ah, when she moved, she moved more ways than one:
The shapes a bright container can contain!
Of her choice virtues only gods should speak,
Or English poets who grew up on Greek
(I'd have them sing in chorus, cheek to cheek).

How well her wishes went! She stroked my chin,
She taught me Turn, and Counter-turn, and Stand;
She taught me Touch, that undulant white skin;
I nibbled meekly from her proffered hand;
She was the sickle; I, poor I, the rake,
Coming behind her for her pretty sake
(But what prodigious mowing we did make).

Love likes a gander, and adores a goose:
Her full lips pursed, the errant note to seize;
She played it quick, she played it light and loose;
My eyes, they dazzled at her flowing knees;
Her several parts could keep a pure repose,
Or one hip quiver with a mobile nose
(She moved in circles, and those circles moved).

Let seed be grass, and grass turn into hay:
I'm martyr to a motion not my own;
What's freedom for? To know eternity.
I swear she cast a shadow white as stone.
But who would count eternity in days?
These old bones live to learn her wanton ways:
(I measure time by how a body sways).

Theodore Roethke

1959

Requiem For The Plantagenet Kings

For whom the possessed sea littered, on both shores,
Ruinous arms; being fired, and for good,
To sound the constitution of just wars,
Men, in their eloquent fashion, understood.

Relieved of soul, the dropping-back of dust,
Their usage, pride, admitted within doors;
At home, under caved chantries, set in trust,
With well-dressed alabaster and proved spurs
They lie; they lie; secure in the decay
Of blood, blood-marks, crowns hacked and coveted,
Before the scouring fires of trial-day
Alight on men; before sleeked groin, gored head,
Budge through the clay and gravel, and the sea
Across daubed rock evacuates its dead.

Geoffrey Hill

1960

The More Loving One

Looking up at the stars, I know quite well
That, for all they care, I can go to hell,
But on earth indifference is the least
We have to dread from man or beast.

How should we like it were stars to burn
With a passion for us we could not return?
If equal affection cannot be,
Let the more loving one be me.

Admirer as I think I am
Of stars that do not give a damn,
I cannot, now I see them, say
I missed one terribly all day.

Were all stars to disappear or die,
I should learn to look at an empty sky
And feel its total dark sublime,
Though this might take me a little time.

W. H. Auden

Song for a Birth or a Death

Last night I saw the savage world
And heard the blood beat up the stair;
The fox's bark, the owl's shrewd pounce,
The crying creatures – all were there,
And men in bed with love and fear.

The slit moon only emphasised
How blood must flow and teeth must grip.
What does the calm light understand,
The light which draws the tide and ship
And drags the owl upon its prey
And human creatures lip to lip?

Last night I watched how pleasure must
Leap from disaster with its will:
The fox's fear, the watch-dog's lust
Know that all matings mean a kill:
And human creatures kissed in trust
Feel the blood throb to death until

The seed is struck, the pleasure's done,
The birds are thronging in the air;
The moon gives way to widespread sun.
Yes but the pain still crouches where
The young fox and the child are trapped
And cries of love are cries of fear.

Elizabeth Jennings

1962

Sonnet in Search of an Author

Nude bodies like peeled logs
sometimes give off a sweetest
odor, man and woman

under the trees in full excess
matching the cushion of

aromatic pine-drift fallen
threaded with trailing woodbine
a sonnet might be made of it

Might be made of it! odor of excess
odor of pine needles, odor of

peeled logs, odor of no odor
other than trailing woodbine that

has no odor, odor of a nude woman
sometimes, odor of a man.

William Carlos Williams

Soap Suds

This brand of soap has the same smell as once in the big
House he visited when he was eight: the walls of the bathroom open
To reveal a lawn where a great yellow ball rolls back through a hoop
To rest at the head of a mallet held in the hands of a child.

And these were the joys of that house: a tower with a telescope;
Two great faded globes, one of the earth, one of the stars;
A stuffed black dog in the hall; a walled garden with bees;
A rabbit warren; a rockery; a vine under glass; the sea.

To which he has now returned. The day of course is fine
And a grown-up voice cries Play! The mallet slowly swings,
Then crack, a great gong booms from the dog-dark hall and the ball
Skims forward through the hoop and then through the next and then

Through hoops where no hoops were and each dissolves in turn
And the grass has grown head-high and an angry voice cries Play!
But the ball is lost and the mallet slipped long since from the hands
Under the running tap that are not the hands of a child.

Louis MacNeice

The Day Lady Died

It is 12:20 in New York a Friday
three days after Bastille day, yes
it is 1959 and I go get a shoeshine
because I will get off the 4:19 in Easthampton
at 7:15 and then go straight to dinner
and I don't know the people who will feed me

I walk up the muggy street beginning to sun
and have a hamburger and a malted and buy
an ugly NEW WORLD WRITING to see what the poets
in Ghana are doing these days
                                        I go on to the bank
and Miss Stillwagon (first name Linda I once heard)
doesn't even look up my balance for once in her life
and in the GOLDEN GRIFFIN I get a little Verlaine
for Patsy with drawings by Bonnard although I do
think of Hesiod, trans. Richmond Lattimore or
Brendan Behan's new play or *Le Balcon* or *Les Nègres*
of Genet, but I don't, I stick with Verlaine
after practically going to sleep with quandariness

and for Mike I just stroll into the PARK LANE
Liquor Store and ask for a bottle of Strega and
then I go back where I came from to 6th Avenue
and the tobacconist in the Ziegfeld Theatre and
casually ask for a carton of Gauloises and a carton
of Picayunes, and a NEW YORK POST with her face on it

and I am sweating a lot by now and thinking of
leaning on the john door in the 5 SPOT
while she whispered a song along the keyboard
to Mal Waldron and everyone and I stopped breathing

Frank O'Hara

23

Filling Station

Oh, but it is dirty!
– this little filling station,
oil-soaked, oil-permeated
to a disturbing, over-all
black translucency.
Be careful with that match!

Father wears a dirty,
oil-soaked monkey suit
that cuts him under the arms,
and several quick and saucy
and greasy sons assist him
(it's a family filling station),
all quite thoroughly dirty.

Do they live in the station?
It has a cement porch
behind the pumps, and on it
a set of crushed and grease-
impregnated wickerwork;
on the wicker sofa
a dirty dog, quite comfy.

Some comic books provide
the only note of color –
of certain color. They lie
upon a big dim doily
draping a taboret
(part of the set), beside
a big hirsute begonia.

Why the extraneous plant?
Why the taboret?
Why, oh why, the doily?
(Embroidered in daisy stitch
with marguerites, I think,
and heavy with gray crochet.)

Somebody embroidered the doily.
Somebody waters the plant,
or oils it, maybe. Somebody
arranges the rows of cans
so that they softly say:
ESSO–SO–SO–SO
to high-strung automobiles.
Somebody loves us all.

Elizabeth Bishop

1966

Three

smell of shit when i lift him he knocks the book from my hand
i hold him up she pulls at my leg the other comes in with a book
he give me his book picks up my book she pulls at his arm
       the other
is pulling my hair i put him down he pulls at my leg she
has taken my book from him and gives it to me i give him
       his book
give her an apple touch the other's hair and open the door

they go down the hall all carrying something

Tom Raworth

Done For!

Take care whom you mix with in life, irresponsible one,
For if you mix with the wrong people
– And you yourself may be one of the wrong people –
If you make love to the wrong person,

In some old building with its fabric of dirt,
As clouds of witchcraft, nitro-glycerine, and cake,
Brush by (one autumn night) still green
From our green sunsets ... and then let hundreds pass, unlit,

They will do you ferocious, indelible harm!
Far beyond anything you can imagine, jazzy sneering one,
And afterwards you'll live in no man's land,
You'll lose your identity, and never get yourself back,
diablotin,

It may have happened already, and as you read this ...
Ah, it *has* happened already. I remember, in an old building;
Clouds which had cut themselves on a sharp winter sunset
(With its smoking stove of frosts to keep it cold) went by,
bleeding.

Rosemary Tonks

Elegy of Fortinbras
for C.M.

Now that we're alone we can talk prince man to man
though you lie on the stairs and see no more than a dead ant
nothing but black sun with broken rays
I could never think of your hands without smiling
and now that they lie on the stone like fallen nests
they are as defenceless as before The end is exactly this
The hands lie apart The sword lies apart The head apart
and the knight's feet in soft slippers

You will have a soldier's funeral without having been a soldier
the only ritual I am acquainted with a little
There will be no candles no singing only cannon-fuses and
      bursts
crepe dragged on the pavement helmets boots artillery horses
      drums drums I know nothing exquisite
those will be my manoeuvres before I start to rule
one has to take the city by the neck and shake it a bit

Anyhow you had to perish Hamlet you were not for life
you believed in crystal notions not in human clay
always twitching as if asleep you hunted chimeras
wolfishly you crunched the air only to vomit
you knew no human thing you did not know even how to
      breathe

Now you have peace Hamlet you accomplished what you
      had to
and you have peace The rest is not silence but belongs to me
you chose the easier part an elegant thrust
but what is heroic death compared with eternal watching
with a cold apple in one's hand on a narrow chair
with a view of the ant-hill and the clock's dial

Adieu prince I have tasks a sewer project
and a decree on prostitutes and beggars

I must also elaborate a better system of prisons
since as you justly said Denmark is a prison
I go to my affairs This night is born
a star named Hamlet We shall never meet
what I shall leave will not be worth a tragedy

It is not for us to greet each other or bid farewell we live on
    archipelagos
and that water these words what can they do what can they
    do prince

Zbigniew Herbert
(Translated by Czeslaw Milosz and Peter Dale Scott)

from Canto CXV

The scientists are in terror
  and the European mind stops
Wyndham Lewis chose blindness
  rather than have his mind stop.
Night under wind mid garofani,
  the petals are almost still
Mozart, Linnaeus, Sulmona,
When one's friends hate each other
  how can there be peace in the world?
Their asperities diverted me in my green time.
A blown husk that is finished
  but the light sings eternal
a pale flare over marshes
  where the salt hay whispers to tide's change
Time, space,
  neither life nor death is the answer.
And of man seeking good,
  doing evil.
In meiner Heimat
  where the dead walked
   and the living were made of cardboard.

Ezra Pound

1970

The Spirit is too Blunt an Instrument

The spirit is too blunt an instrument
to have made this baby.
Nothing so unskilful as human passions
could have managed the intricate
exacting particulars: the tiny
blind bones with their manipulating tendons,
the knee and the knucklebones, the resilient
fine meshings of ganglia and vertebrae,
the chain of the difficult spine.

Observe the distinct eyelashes and sharp crescent
fingernails, the shell-like complexity
of the ear, with its firm involutions
concentric in miniature to minute
ossicles. Imagine the
infinitesimal capillaries, the flawless connections
of the lungs, the invisible neural filaments
through which the completed body
already answers to the brain.

Then name any passion or sentiment
possessed of the simplest accuracy.
No, no desire or affection could have done
with practice what habit
has done perfectly, indifferently,
through the body's ignorant precision.
It is left to the vagaries of the mind to invent
love and despair and anxiety
and their pain.

Anne Stevenson

Poems For Blok 1

Your name is a – bird in my hand
a piece of – ice on the tongue
one single movement of the lips.
Your name is: five signs,
a ball caught in flight, a
silver bell in the mouth

a stone, cast in a quiet pool
makes the splash of your name, and
the sound is in the clatter of
night hooves, loud as a thunderclap
or it speaks straight into my forehead,
shrill as the click of a cocked gun.

Your name – how impossible, it
is a kiss in the eyes on
motionless eyelashes, chill and sweet.
Your name is a kiss of snow
a gulp of icy spring water, blue
as a dove. About your name is: sleep.

Marina Tsvetayeva
(Translated by Elaine Feinstein)

1972

Anahorish

My 'place of clear water',
the first hill in the world
where springs washed into
the shiny grass

and darkened cobbles
in the bed of the lane.
Anahorish, soft gradient
of consonant, vowel-meadow,

after-image of lamps
swung through the yards
on winter evenings.
With pails and barrows

those mound-dwellers
go waist-deep in mist
to break the light ice
at wells and dunghills.

Seamus Heaney

19 73

Dolphin

My Dolphin, you only guide me by surprise,
captive as Racine, the man of craft,
drawn through his maze of iron composition
by the incomparable wandering voice of Phèdre.
When I was troubled in mind, you made for my body
caught in its hangman's-knot of sinking lines,
the glassy bowing and scraping of my will . . . .
I have sat and listened to too many
words of the collaborating muse,
and plotted perhaps too freely with my life,
not avoiding injury to others,
not avoiding injury to myself –
to ask compassion . . . this book, half fiction,
an eelnet made by man for the eel fighting –

my eyes have seen what my hand did.

Robert Lowell

The Old Fools

What do they think has happened, the old fools,
To make them like this? Do they somehow suppose
It's more grown-up when your mouth hangs open and drools,
And you keep on pissing yourself, and can't remember
Who called this morning? Or that, if they only chose,
They could alter things back to when they danced all night,
Or went to their wedding, or sloped arms some September?
Or do they fancy there's really been no change,
And they've always behaved as if they were crippled or tight,
Or sat through days of thin continuous dreaming
Watching light move? If they don't (and they can't), it's strange:
                Why aren't they screaming?

At death, you break up: the bits that were you
Start speeding away from each other for ever
With no one to see. It's only oblivion, true:
We had it before, but then it was going to end,
And was all the time merging with a unique endeavour
To bring to bloom the million-petalled flower
Of being here. Next time you can't pretend
There'll be anything else. And these are the first signs:
Not knowing how, not hearing who, the power
Of choosing gone. Their looks show that they're for it:
Ash hair, toad hands, prune face dried into lines –
                How can they ignore it?

Perhaps being old is having lighted rooms
Inside your head, and people in them, acting.
People you know, yet can't quite name; each looms
Like a deep loss restored, from known doors turning,
Setting down a lamp, smiling from a stair, extracting
A known book from the shelves; or sometimes only
The rooms themselves, chairs and a fire burning,
The blown bush at the window, or the sun's
Faint friendliness on the wall some lonely
Rain-ceased midsummer evening. That is where they live:
Not here and now, but where all happened once.
                This is why they give

An air of baffled absence, trying to be there
Yet being here. For the rooms grow farther, leaving
Incompetent cold, the constant wear and tear
Of taken breath, and them crouching below
Extinction's alp, the old fools, never perceiving
How near it is. This must be what keeps them quiet:
The peak that stays in view wherever we go
For them is rising ground. Can they never tell
What is dragging them back, and how it will end? Not at night?
Not when the strangers come? Never, throughout
The whole hideous inverted childhood? Well,
                We shall find out.

Philip Larkin

The God Abandons Antony

At midnight, when suddenly you hear
an invisible procession going by
with exquisite music, voices,
don't mourn your luck that's failing now,
work gone wrong, your plans
all proving deceptive – don't mourn them uselessly:
as one long prepared, and full of courage,
say goodbye to her, to Alexandria who is leaving.
Above all, don't fool yourself, don't say
it was a dream, your ears deceived you:
don't degrade yourself with empty hopes like these.
As one long prepared, and full of courage,
as is right for you who were given this kind of city,
go firmly to the window
and listen with deep emotion,
but not with the whining, the pleas of a coward;
listen – your final pleasure – to the voices,
to the exquisite music of that strange procession,
and say goodbye to her, to the Alexandria you are losing.

C. P. Cavafy
(Translated by E. Keeley and P. Sherrard)

1976

Voice

I have always laughed
when someone spoke of a young writer
"finding his voice." I took it
literally: had he lost his voice?
Had he thrown it and had it
not returned? Or perhaps they
were referring to his newspaper
The Village Voice? He's trying
to find his *Voice*.
            What isn't
funny is that so many young writers
seem to have found this notion
credible: they set off in search
of their voice, as if it were
a single thing, a treasure
difficult to find but worth
the effort. I never thought
such a thing existed. Until
recently. Now I know it does.
I hope I never find mine. I
wish to remain a phony the rest of my life.

Ron Padgett

1977

Loch Thom

1

Just for the sake of recovering
I walked backward from fifty-six
Quick years of age wanting to see,
And managed not to trip or stumble
To find Loch Thom and turned round
To see the stretch of my childhood
Before me. Here is the loch. The same
Long-beaked cry curls across
The heather-edges of the water held
Between the hills a boyhood's walk
Up from Greenock. It is the morning.

And I am here with my mammy's
Bramble jam scones in my pocket.
The Firth is miles and I have come
Back to find Loch Thom maybe
In this light does not recognise me.

This is a lonely freshwater loch.
No farms on the edge. Only
Heather grouse-moor stretching
Down to Greenock and One Hope
Street or stretching away across
Into the blue moors of Ayrshire.

2

And almost I am back again
Wading the heather down to the edge
To sit. The minnows go by in shoals
Like iron-filings in the shallows.
My mother is dead. My father is dead
And all the trout I used to know
Leaping from their sad rings are dead.

3

I drop my crumbs into the shallow
Weed for the minnows and pinheads.
You see that I will have to rise
And turn round and get back where
My running age will slow for a moment
To let me on. It is a colder
Stretch of water than I remember.

The curlew's cry travelling still
Kills me fairly. In front of me
The grouse flurry and settle. GOBACK
GOBACK GOBACK FAREWELL LOCH THOM.

W.S. Graham

1978

Poem X

From the sequence 'Twenty-one Love Poems'

Your dog, tranquil and innocent, dozes through
our cries, our murmured dawn conspiracies
our telephone calls. She knows—what can she know?
If in my human arrogance I claim to read
her eyes, I find there only my own animal thoughts:
that creatures must find each other for bodily comfort,
that voices of the psyche drive through the flesh
further than the dense brain could have foretold,
that the planetary nights are growing cold for those
on the same journey who want to touch
one creature-traveler clear to the end;
that without tenderness, we are in hell.

Adrienne Rich

February 17th

A lamb could not get born. Ice wind
Out of a downpour dishclout sunrise. The mother
Lay on the mudded slope. Harried, she got up
And the blackish lump bobbed at her back-end
Under her tail. After some hard galloping,
Some manoeuvring, much flapping of the backward
Lump head of the lamb looking out,
I caught her with a rope. Laid her, head uphill,
And examined the lamb. A blood-ball swollen
Tight in its black felt, its mouth gap
Squashed crooked, tongue stuck out, black-purple,
Strangled by its mother. I felt inside,
Past the noose of mother-flesh, into the slippery
Muscled tunnel, fingering for a hoof,
Right back to the porthole of the pelvis.
But there was no hoof. He had stuck his head out too early
And his feet could not follow. He should have
Felt his way, tip-toe, his toes
Tucked up under his nose
For a safe landing. So I kneeled wrestling
With her groans. No hand could squeeze past
The lamb's neck into her interior
To hook a knee. I roped that baby head
And hauled till she cried out and tried
To get up and I saw it was useless. I went
Two miles for the injection and a razor.
Sliced the lamb's throat-strings, levered with a knife
Between the vertebrae and brought the head off
To stare at its mother, its pipes sitting in the mud
With all earth for a body. Then pushed
The neck stump right back in, and as I pushed
She pushed. She pushed crying and I pushed gasping.
And the strength
Of the birth push and the push of my thumb
Against that wobbly vertebra were deadlock,
A to-fro futility. Till I forced
A hand past and got a knee. Then like

Pulling myself to the ceiling with one finger
Hooked in a loop, timing my effort
To her birth push groans, I pulled against
The corpse that would not come. Till it came.
And after it the long, sudden, yolk-yellow
Parcel of life
In a smoking slither of oils and soups and syrups –
And the body lay born, beside the hacked-off head.

Ted Hughes

Aspen Tree

ASPEN TREE your leaves glance white into the dark.
My mother's hair was never white.

Dandelion, so green is the Ukraine.
My yellow-haired mother did not come home.

Rain cloud, above the well do you hover?
My quiet mother weeps for everyone.

Round star, you wind the golden loop.
My mother's heart was ripped by lead.

Oaken door, who lifted you off your hinges?
My gentle mother cannot return.

Paul Celan
(Translated by Michael Hamburger)

1981

Timer

Gold survives the fire that's hot enough
to make you ashes in a standard urn.
An envelope of coarse official buff
contains your wedding ring which wouldn't burn.

Dad told me I'd to tell them at St James's
that the ring should go in the incinerator.
That 'eternity' inscribed with both their names is
his surety that they'd be together, 'later'.

I signed for the parcelled clothing as the son,
the cardy, apron, pants, bra, dress

the clerk phoned down: 6-8-8-3-1?
Has she still her ring on? (Slight pause) *Yes*!

It's on my warm palm now, your burnished ring!

I feel your ashes, head, arms, breasts, womb, legs,
sift through its circle slowly, like that thing
you used to let me watch to time the eggs.

Tony Harrison

The Killer Snails

The killer snails
Have slung their silver trails
Along the doormat, out across the lawn,
Under the bushes
Where the alarming thrushes
Give night its notice, making way for dawn,
And the obliging lizards drop their tails.

On webs of dew
The spiders stir their pots of glue
And drag their quartered victims to the shade.
Soaked in their rugs
Of grass and moss the slugs
Wind up another night of sluggish trade
And young ingredients get into a stew.

The sorrel bends.
The path fades out but never ends
Where brambles clutch and bracken wipes your feet.
It goes in rings.
Its mind's on other things.
Its way and its intentions never meet.
Meetings of friends?
It gives no undertaking. It depends.

James Fenton

Watching for Dolphins

In the summer months on every crossing to Piraeus
One noticed that certain passengers soon rose
From seats in the packed saloon and with serious
Looks and no acknowledgement of a common purpose
Passed forward through the small door into the bows
To watch for dolphins. One saw them lose

Every other wish. Even the lovers
Turned their desires on the sea, and a fat man
Hung with equipment to photograph the occasion
Stared like a saint, through sad bi-focals; others,
Hopeless themselves, looked to the children for they
Would see dolphins if anyone would. Day after day

Or on their last opportunity all gazed
Undecided whether a flat calm were favourable
Or a sea the sun and the wind between them raised
To a likeness of dolphins. Were gulls a sign, that fell
Screeching from the sky or over an unremarkable place
Sat in a silent school? Every face

After its character implored the sea.
All, unaccustomed, wanted epiphany,
Praying the sky would clang and the abused Aegean
Reverberate with cymbal, gong and drum.
We could not imagine more prayer, and had they then
On the waves, on the climax of our longing come

Smiling, snub-nosed, domed like satyrs, oh
We should have laughed and lifted the children up
Stranger to stranger, pointing how with a leap
They left their element, three or four times, centred
On grace, and heavily and warm re-entered,
Looping the keel. We should have felt them go

Further and further into the deep parts. But soon
We were among the great tankers, under their chains
In black water. We had not seen the dolphins
But woke, blinking. Eyes cast down
With no admission of disappointment the company
Dispersed and prepared to land in the city.

David Constantine

Don't Talk to Me about Bread

she kneads
deep into the night
and the whey-coloured dough

springy and easy and yielding to her will

is revenge. Like a rival,
dough toys with her. Black-brown hands in the belly
bringing forth a sigh.

She slaps it, slaps it double with fists
with heel of hand applies the punishment
not meant for bread

and the bitch on the table sighs
and exhales a little spray of flour
a satisfied breath of white

on her hand

mocking the colour
robbing hands of their power
as they go through the motions, kneading…
She listens for the sigh which haunts

from the wrong side of her own door
from this wanton cheat of dough
this whey-faced bitch rising up

in spite of her fight, rising up
her nipples, her belly, rising up
two legs, dear god, in a blackwoman's rage…

Laughing at her, all laughing at her:
giggling bitch, abandoned house, and Man
still promising from afar what men promise…

Hands come to life again: knife
in the hand, the belly ripped open, and she smears

white lard and butter, she sprinkles
a little obeah of flour and curses to stop up the wound.

Then she doubles the bitch up
with cuffs, wrings her like washing
till she's the wrong shape

and the tramp lets out a damp, little sigh
a little hiss of white
enjoying it.

E. A. Markham

1985

Mock Orange

It is not the moon, I tell you.
It is these flowers
lighting the yard.

I hate them.
I hate them as I hate sex,
the man's mouth
sealing my mouth, the man's
paralyzing body—

and the cry that always escapes,
the low, humiliating
premise of union—

In my mind tonight
I hear the question and pursuing answer
fused in one sound
that mounts and mounts and then
is split into the old selves,
the tired antagonisms. Do you see?
We were made fools of.
And the scent of mock orange
drifts through the window.

How can I rest?
How can I be content
when there is still
that odor in the world?

Louise Glück

We Love Life Whenever We Can

We love life whenever we can.

We dance and throw up a minaret or raise palm trees for the violets
growing between two martyrs.

We love life whenever we can.

We steal a thread from a silk-worm to weave a sky and a fence for our
journey.

We open the garden gate for the jasmine to walk into the street as a
beautiful day.

We love life whenever we can.

Wherever we settle we grow fast-growing plants, wherever we settle
we harvest a murdered man.

We blow into the flute the colour of far away, of far away, we draw on
the dust in the passage the neighing of a horse.

And we write our names in the form of stones. Lightning, brighten the
night for us, brighten the night a little.

We love life whenever we can.

Mahmoud Darwish
(Translated by Abdullah Al-Udhari)

1987

Meeting the British

We met the British in the dead of winter.
The sky was lavender

and the snow lavender-blue.
I could hear, far below,

the sound of two streams coming together
(both were frozen over)

and, no less strange,
myself calling out in French

across that forest-
clearing. Neither General Jeffrey Amherst

nor Colonel Henry Bouquet
could stomach our willow-tobacco.

As for the unusual
scent when the Colonel shook out his hand-

kerchief: *C'est la lavande,*
une fleur mauve comme le ciel.

They gave us six fishhooks
and two blankets embroidered with smallpox.

Paul Muldoon

Eden Rock

They are waiting for me somewhere beyond Eden Rock:
My father, twenty-five, in the same suit
Of Genuine Irish Tweed, his terrier Jack
Still two years old and trembling at his feet.

My mother, twenty-three, in a sprigged dress
Drawn at the waist, ribbon in her straw hat,
Has spread the stiff white cloth over the grass.
Her hair, the colour of wheat, takes on the light.

She pours tea from a Thermos, the milk straight
From an old H.P. Sauce bottle, a screw
Of paper for a cork; slowly sets out
The same three plates, the tin cups painted blue.

The sky whitens as if lit by three suns.
My mother shades her eyes and looks my way
Over the drifted stream. My father spins
A stone along the water. Leisurely,

They beckon to me from the other bank.
I hear them call, 'See where the stream-path is!
Crossing is not as hard as you might think.'

I had not thought that it would be like this.

Charles Causley

Family Album

Loneliness – huge, suddenly menacing
and no one is left here who knows me anymore:
the Little League coach,
his TV repair truck and stinking cigars
and Saul the Butcherman
and the broken arm that fell out of the apple tree
dead
dead or gone south to die warm

The little boy with mittens and dog
posing on the stoop –
he isn't me;
and the young couple in polo shirts, ready to pop
with their firstborn
four pages on in shortshorts and beatnik top
showing her figure off at 16 …
1955 is in an attic bookcase
spine cracked and pages falling out

Willow and plum tree
green pods from maple whirling down to the sidewalk …
Only the guy at the hot dog stand since when
maybe remembers me,
or at least looks twice

But the smushfaced bus from New York, dropping
them off at night along
these avenues of brick somber as the dead child
and crimes of old mayors
lets off no one I know, or want to

Warm grass and dragonflies –
O, my heart

August Kleinzahler

1990

No Ordinary Thing

Small days walk on stilts.
Mother Sally dances in your childhood eye.
Masquerade magic rivets you to a window,
eyes wide enough to accommodate a ritual,
and what the drum doing to you
will not be mentioned in your passport.

Small days get high on fruit.
Your young mouth dismembers a starapple
that stains lips with innocent semen.
I conjure you, little red girl
back in a tropical time,
willing your own nipples into bud.
Rudeness is part of your heritage.
Your mother, playing the piano,
scolds you for repeating a brazen folksong.
You discover geography between your legs
but go to bed with Enid Blyton.

Now wrap a warm scarf around your neck
and think of the tropical riddles that reside
beneath your winter coat.

No ordinary thing, my love.

John Agard

1991

Those Who Carry

Those who carry pianos
to the tenth floor
wardrobes and coffins
an old man who with a bundle of wood limps
    beyond the horizon
a woman with a hump of nettles
a madwoman pushing a pram
full of vodka bottles
they will all be lifted
like a gull's feather like a dry leaf
like an eggshell a scrap of newspaper

Blessed are those who carry
for they shall be lifted

Anna Kamienska
(Translated by Tomasz Krzeszowski and Desmond Graham)

A Marriage

We met
    under a shower
of bird-notes.
    Fifty years passed,
love's moment
    in a world in
servitude to time.
    She was young;
I kissed with my eyes
    closed and opened
them on her wrinkles.
    'Come' said death,
choosing her as his
    partner for
the last dance. And she,
    who in life
had done everything
    with a bird's grace,
opened her bill now
    for the shedding
of one sigh no
    heavier than a feather.

R.S. Thomas

Shantung

It's true that anyone can fall
in love with anyone at all.
Later, they can't. Ouf, ouf.

How much mascara washes away each day
and internationally, making the blue one black.
Come on everybody. Especially you girls.

Each day I think of something about dying.
Does everybody? do they think too, I mean.
My friends! some answers. Gently
unstrap my wristwatch. Lay it face down.

Denise Riley

Peacocks

I would be Adam
leafless in the garden
with all my ribs about me
one day more.
(His days I mean: my aeons.)
One more day
His voice be off the air
a heavenly silence
in which to find my feet
and clench my fingers
to grasp the Situation.

I don't like it.

To be creation's clown
a six-day wonder,
a ten-toed biped
with this bag of pebbles
that wobble when I walk.

He should have held His breath.
Five days was plenty.

Earth, sun, flesh, fowl; then feet up.

Make feathers fly, and finish.

Peacocks. Full stop.

Peacocks was really great.

Sean Rafferty

The Fishing Party

Because he loves off-duty policemen and their murderers
Christ is still seen walking on the water of Lough Neagh,
Whose fingers created bluebottles, meadow-browns, red
Admirals, painted ladies, fire-flies, and are tying now
Woodcock hackles around hooks, lamb's wool, badger fur

Until about his head swarm artificial flies and their names,
Dark Mackerel, Gravel Bed, Greenwell's Glory, Soldier
Palmer, Coachman, Water Cricket, Orange Grouse, Barm,
Without snagging in his hair or ceasing to circle above
Policemen turned by gunmen into fishermen for ever.

Michael Longley

It Allows a Portrait in Line Scan at Fifteen

He retains a slight 'Martian' accent, from the years of single phrases.

He no longer hugs to disarm. It is gradually allowing him affection.

It does not allow proportion. Distress is absolute, shrieking, and runs him at
frantic speed through crashing doors.

He likes cyborgs. Their taciturn power, with his intonation.

It still runs him around the house, alone in the dark, cooing and laughing.

He can read about soils, populations and New Zealand. On neutral topics
he's illiterate.

Arnie Schwarzenegger is an actor. He isn't a cyborg really, is he, Dad?

He lives on forty acres, with animals and trees, and used to draw it continually.

He knows the map of Earth's fertile soils, and can draw it freehand.

He can only lie in a panicked shout *SorrySorryIdidn'tdoit!* warding off
conflict with others and himself.

When he ran away constantly it was to the greengrocers to worship stacked fruit.

His favourite country was the Ukraine: it is nearly all deep fertile soil.

Giggling, he climbed all over the dim Freudian psychiatrist who told us how
autism resulted from 'refrigerator' parents.

When asked to smile, he photographs a rictus-smile on his face.

It long forbade all naturalistic films. They were Adult movies.

If they (that is, he) *are bad the police will put them in hospital.*

He sometimes drew the farm amid Chinese or Balinese rice terraces.

When a runaway, he made uproar in the police station, playing at three times
adult speed.

Only animated films were proper. *Who Framed Roger Rabbit* then authorised
the rest.

Phrases spoken to him he would take as teaching, and repeat,

When he worshipped fruit, he screamed as if poisoned when it was fed to
him.

A one-word first conversation: *Blane. – Yes! Plane, that's right, baby! – Blane.*

He has forgotten nothing, and remembers the precise quality of experiences.

It requires rulings: *Is stealing very playing up, as bad as murder?*

He counts at a glance, not looking. And he has never been lost.

When he ate only nuts and dried fruit, words were for dire emergencies.

He knows all the breeds of fowls, and the counties of Ireland.

He'd begun to talk, then returned to babble, then silence. It withdrew speech
for years.

When he took your hand, it was to work it, as a multi-purpose tool.
He is anger's mirror, and magnifies any near him, raging it down.
It still won't allow him fresh fruit, or orange juice with bits in it.
He swam in the midwinter dam at night. It had no rules about cold.
He was terrified of thunder and finally cried as if in explanation *It – angry!*
He grilled an egg he'd broken into bread. Exchanges of soil knowledge are
    called landtalking.
He lives in objectivity. I was sure Bell's palsy would leave my face only when
    he said it had begun to.
Don't say word! when he was eight forbade the word 'autistic' in his presence.
Bantering questions about girlfriends cause a terrified look and blocked ears.
He sometimes centred the farm in a furrowed American midwest.
Eye contact, Mum! means he truly wants attention. It dislikes I- contact.
He is equitable and kind, and only ever a little jealous. It was a relief when
    that little arrived.
He surfs, bowls, walks for miles. For many years he hasn't trailed his left arm
    while running.
I gotta get smart! looking terrified into the years. *I gotta get smart!*

Les Murray

11:00: Baldovan

Base Camp. Horizontal sleet. Two small boys
have raised the steel flag of the 20 terminus:

me and Ross Mudie are going up the Hilltown
for the first time ever on our own.

I'm weighing up my spending power: the shillings,
tanners, black pennies, florins with bald kings,

the cold blazonry of a half-crown, threepenny bits
like thick cogs, making them chank together in my pockets.

I plan to buy comics,
sweeties, and magic tricks.

However, I am obscurely worried, as usual,
over matters of procedure, the protocol of travel,

and keep asking Ross the same questions:
where we should sit, when to pull the bell, even

if we have enough money for the fare,
whispering, *Are ye sure? Are ye sure?*

I cannot know the little good it will do me;
the bus will let us down in another country

with the wrong streets and streets that suddenly forget
their names at crossroads or in building-sites

and where no one will have heard of the sweets we ask for
and the man will shake the coins from our fists onto the counter

and call for his wife to come through, come through and see this
and if we ever make it home again, the bus

will draw into the charred wreck of itself

and we will enter the land at the point we left off

only our voices sound funny and all the houses are gone
and the rain tastes like kelly and black waves fold in

very slowly at the foot of Macalpine Road
and our sisters and mothers are fifty years dead.

Don Paterson

1998

Gorgeous –
yet another Brighton poem

The summer's here.
Down to the beach
to swim and lounge and swim again.
Gorgeous bodies young and old.
Me too. Just gorgeous. Just feeling good
and happy and so at ease in the world.

And come early evening a red sun setting,
the sea all silky,
small gentle surges along its near still surface.

And later
the new moon hung over the sea,
a stippled band of gold across the black water,
tiger's eye.

I walk home.
The air so soft and warm,
like fur brushing my body.

The dictionary says
"**gorgeous** – adorned with rich and brilliant colours,
sumptuously splendid, showy, magnificent, dazzling."

That's right.

Lee Harwood

We Are Not Stones

Darkly-harnessed light will fall like a shawl
and be the hunky-dory
death of us all. A hawk-wing death,
a shrike strike death, a death in a lair.
This mossy path, frilled with feldspar
to prick your pearly toes, fresh from the marigolds,
the little stile not squeaking now, lubricated
hinges, hymns to the silence of adult interference,
new sunken screwheads glinty in sunlight,
the death of the white linen: our cot-death.
It was all, all of it, all for us, from the wonders
of our mysterious heaven
to the trout's opal seed-sac bubbling with jewels.
The water was anointment water,
a cool upland baptism. You, you
were Delilah and Mary-of-the-tears,
of the unspoiled lips lapping rushing whitewater.
Milton was a blind man and we knew nothing of him.
Paradise Lost to the ears of his daughter.
Where are they now, our camps of wild primrose?
Now we are adults too, all grown-up.
You're there, I'm here, miles from our happiness.
We are not stone, but we are in the grinder.
Everything is lost, and we are dust and done for.

Barry MacSweeney

2000

Terminal

Didn't you get my card?
We none of us, you see, knew we were coming
until the bus was actually pulling out of the terminal.
I gazed a little sadly at the rubber of my shoes'
soles, finding it wanting.

I got kind of frenzied after the waiting
had stopped, but now am cool as a suburban garden
in some lost city. When it came time for my speech
I could think of nothing, of course.
I gave a little talk about the onion–how its flavor
inspires us, its shape informs our architecture.
There were so many other things I wanted to say, too,
but, dandified, I couldn't strut,
couldn't sit down for all the spit and polish.
Now it's your turn to say something about the wall
in the garden. It can be anything.

John Ashbery

The Race Industry

The coconuts have got the jobs.

The race industry is a growth industry.

We despairing, they careering.

We want more peace they want more police.

The Uncle Toms are getting paid.

The race industry is a growth industry.

We say sisters and brothers don't fear.

They will do anything for the Mayor.

The coconuts have got the jobs.

The race industry is a growth industry.

They're looking for victims and poets to rent.

They represent me without my consent.

The Uncle Toms are getting paid.

The race industry is a growth industry.

In suits they dither in fear of anarchy.

They take our sufferings and earn a salary.

Steal our souls and make their documentaries.

Inform daily on our community.

Without Black suffering they'd have no jobs.

Without our dead they'd have no office.

Without our tears they'd have no drink.

If they stopped sucking we could get justice.

The coconuts are getting paid.

Men, women and Brixton are being betrayed.

Benjamin Zephaniah

Ghalib's Ghazal

Not all, only a few –
    disguised as tulips, as roses –
      return from ashes.
What possibilities
    has the earth forever
      covered, what faces?

Time ago I too could recall
    those moon-lit nights,
      wine on the Saqi's roof –
But Time's shelved them now
    in its niche, in
      Memory's dim places.

Let me weep, let this blood
    flow from my eyes.
      She is leaving.
These tears, I'll say, have
    lit my eyes, two candles
      for love's darkest spaces.

What isn't his?
    He is Sleep, is Peace, is Night,
      mere mortal become god
when your hair lies scattered,
    shining, on his shoulder,
      he now one whom nothing effaces.

Wine, a giver of life! Hold the glass.
    The palm's lines, as one, will
      rush to life –
Here's my hand, its
    life-line beating, here
      Look! the glass it raises.

Man is numbed to pain
   when he's sorrow-beaten.
      Sorrows, piled up, ease pain.
Grief crushed me so
   again and again it became
      the pain that pain erases.

World, take note, should Ghalib
   keep weeping, you'll see
      only a wilderness
where you built
   your terraced cities,
      your marble palaces.

Agha Shahid Ali

Acknowledgements

The editors and publishers gratefully acknowledge permissions to use copyright material in this book as follows:

JOHN AGARD: to the author for 'No Ordinary Thing' from *Lovelines For A Goat Born Lady* (Serpent's Tail, 1990). AGHA SHAHID ALI: to W.W. Norton for 'Ghalib's Ghazal' from *Rooms Are Never Finished* (W.W. Norton, 2002). JOHN ASHBERY: to Carcanet Press for 'Terminal' from *Your Name Here* (Carcanet, 2000). WH AUDEN: to Faber and Faber for 'The More Loving One' from *Collected Poems* (Faber, 1976). ELIZABETH BISHOP: to Farrar, Strauss and Giroux for 'Filling Station' from *Complete Poems* (Chatto & Windus, 1991). CHARLES CAUSLEY: to David Higham Associates for 'Eden Rock' from *A Field of Vision* (Macmillan, 1988). C.P. CAVAFY: to Random House Group Ltd for 'The God Abandons Antony' from *Collected Poems* translated by E Keeley and P Sherrard (Chatto and Windus, 1975). PAUL CELAN: to Anvil Press for 'Aspen Tree' from *Poems of Paul Celan* translated by Michael Hamburger (Anvil, 1988). DAVID CONSTANTINE: to Bloodaxe Books for 'Watching for Dolphins' from *Selected Poems* (Bloodaxe, 1991). MAHMOUD DARWISH: to Abdullah Al-Udhari for 'We Love Life Whenever we Can' from *Modern Poetry of the Arab World* (Penguin, 1986). WILLIAM EMPSON: to Penguin for 'Chinese Ballad' from *The Complete Poems* (Allen Lane, Penguin Press, 2000). JAMES FENTON: to Peters, Fraser & Dunlop Group Limited for 'The Killer Snails' from *The Memory of War and Children In Exile* (Penguin, 1983). LOUISE GLUCK: to Carcanet press for 'Mock Orange' from *First Five Books of Poems* (Carcanet, 1997). W.S. GRAHAM: to Margaret Snow for 'Loch Thom' from *Collected Poems* (Faber, 1979). THOM GUNN: to Faber and Faber for 'Wind in the Street' from *Collected Poems* (Faber, 1993). TONY HARRISON: to Gordon Dickerson for 'Timer' from *Selected Poems* (Penguin, 1984). LEE HARWOOD: to the author for 'Gorgeous – yet another Brighton poem' from *Morning Light* (Slow Dancer, 1998). SEAMUS HEANEY: to Faber and Faber for 'Anahorish' from *Opened Ground: Poems 1966-1996* (Faber, 1998). ZBIGNIEW HERBERT: to Penguin for 'Elegy of Fortinbras' from *Selected Poems* (Penguin, 1968). GEOFFREY HILL: to Penguin for 'Requiem for the Plantagenet Kings' from *Collected Poems* (Penguin, 1985). TED HUGHES: to Faber and Faber for 'February 17th' from *New Selected Poems 1957-1994* (Faber, 1995). ELIZABETH JENNINGS: to David Higham Associates for 'Song for a Birth or a Death' from *New Collected Poems* (Carcanet, 2002). ANNA KAMIENSKA: to Flambard Press for 'Those Who Carry' from *Two Darknesses* translated by T.P. Krzeszowski & D. Graham (Flambard Press, 1991). AUGUST KLEINZAHLER: to Moyer Bell for 'Family Album' from *Earthquake Weather* (Moyer Bell, 1989). PHILIP LARKIN: to Faber and Faber for 'The Old Fools' from *Collected Poems* (Faber, 1988). ROBERT LOWELL: to Faber and Faber for 'Dolphin' from *Poems, selected by Michael Hoffman* (Faber, 2001). MICHAEL

LONGLEY: to Random House Group Ltd for 'The Fishing Party' from *Selected Poems* (Jonathan Cape, 1998). LOUIS MACNEICE: to David Higham Associates for 'Soap Suds' from *The Collected Poems* (Faber, 1966). BARRY MACSWEENEY: to the Estate of Barry MacSweeney for 'We Are Not Stones' from *Pearl In The Silver Morning* (Poetical Histories, 1999). E.A. MARKHAM: to Anvil Press for 'Don't Talk To Me About Bread' from *Human Rites: Selected Poems 1970-1982* (Anvil, 1984). MARIANNE MOORE: to Faber and Faber for 'The Sycamore' from *Complete Poems* (Faber, 1984). LES MURRAY: to Carcanet Press for 'It Allows A Portrait In Line Scan At Fifteen' from *New Collected Poems* (Carcanet, 2003). FRANK O'HARA: to Carcanet Press for 'The Day Lady Died' from *Selected Poems* (Carcanet, 1991). RON PADGETT: to the author for 'Voice' from *New And Selected Poems* (David R. Godine, 1995). DON PATERSON: to Faber and Faber for '11.00: Baldovan' from *God's Gift to Women* (Faber, 1997). EZRA POUND: to Faber and Faber for 'from CXV' from *The Cantos* (Faber, 1986). SEAN RAFFERTY: to Christian Coupe for 'Peacocks' from *Collected Poems* (Carcanet, 1995). TOM RAWORTH: to Carcanet Press for 'Three' from *Collected Poems* (Carcanet, 2003). ADRIENNE RICH: to W.W. Norton for 'X, Twenty-One Love Poems' from *The Dream of a Common Language* (W.W. Norton, 1978). DENISE RILEY: to Reality Street Editions for 'Shantung' from *Selected Poems* (Reality Street Editions, 2000). THEODORE ROETHKE: to Faber and Faber for 'I Knew a Woman' from *Selected Poems* (Faber, 1969). STEVIE SMITH: to James MacGibbon Estate for 'I Remember' from *Selected Poems* (Penguin, 1978). WALLACE STEVENS: to Faber and Faber for 'The Poem That Took The Place of a Mountain' from *The Collected Poems* (Faber, 1955). ANNE STEVENSON: to Bloodaxe Books for 'The Spirit Is Too Blunt An Instrument' from *The Collected Poems: 1955-1995* (Bloodaxe, 2000). R.S. THOMAS: to Bloodaxe Books for 'A Marriage' from *Mass for Hard Times* (Bloodaxe, 1992). ROSEMARY TONKS: unable to trace copyright holders. MARINA TSVETAYEVA: to Carcanet Press for 'Poems for Blok Part 1' from *Selected Poems* translated by Elaine Feinstein (Carcanet, 1999). WILLIAM CARLOS WILLIAMS: to Carcanet Press for 'Sonnet In Search Of An Author' from *Collected Poems II 1939-1962* (Carcanet, 2000). BENJAMIN ZEPHANIAH to Bloodaxe Books for 'The Race Industry' from *Too Black Too Strong* (Bloodaxe, 2001).

Every effort has been made to contact all copyright holders. The publishers will be grateful of any notification of additions that should be incorporated in the next edition of this volume.